THE Horribly FUNNY JOKE BOOK

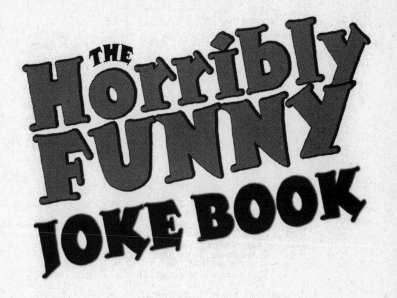

THE Horribly FUNNY JOKE BOOK

by Kay Woodward

Illustrated by Chris Fisher

SCHOLASTIC

Scholastic Children's Books,
Euston House, 24 Eversholt Street,
London NW1 1DB, UK
a division of Scholastic Ltd

London ~ New York ~ Toronto ~ Sydney ~ Auckland
Mexico City ~ New Delhi ~ Hong Kong

First published in the UK by Scholastic Ltd, 2006

This collection copyright © Kay Woodward, 2006
Illustrations copyright © Chris Fisher, 2006

10 digit ISBN 0 439 95071 6
13 digit ISBN 978 0439 95071 8

Printed and bound by Nørhaven Paperback A/S, Denmark

10 9 8 7 6 5 4 3 2 1

Papers used by Scholastic Children's Books are made from wood grown in
sustainable forests.

CONTENTS

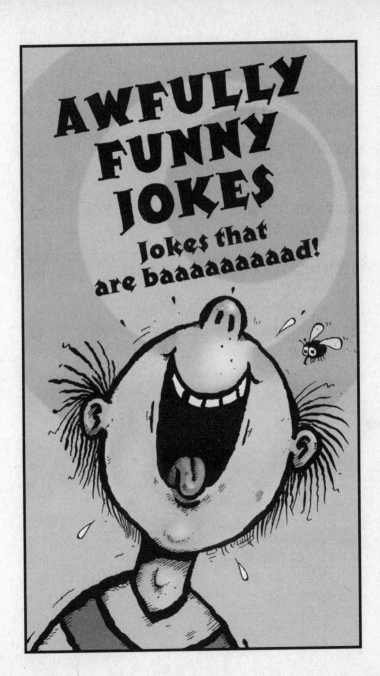

What do you get if you drop a piano down a lift shaft?
A flat miner.

What's fluorescent, sweet and helps children to cross the road?
A lollypop lady.

Which sport do chefs like to play?
Bowls.

What's the pointiest
sweet in a sweetshop?
A spearmint.

What's got a
bottom at the top?
A toilet.

What do you call
an alien with
three eyes?
Aliiien.

What do snowmen sing at parties?
Freeze a jolly good fellow!

What happened when the boy went to buy a pair of camouflage trousers?
He couldn't find any!

Why did the computer go to the doctor's?
It had a nasty virus.

Why did the snooker player feel off colour?
He wasn't getting enough greens.

What do you say to a mountaineer who's sitting on top of Everest?
Hi!

Why did the satsuma go to the doctor's?
He wasn't peeling too well.

Did you hear about the poetic alien?
He wrote uni-verse.

What do double agents play when they go on holiday?
I spy.

Did you hear about the Christmas cake that was whisked away by the police without warning?
It was full of dangerous currants.

Why did the clown throw cream pies at the audience?
It was jest for fun.

What happens when you throw eggs at a Dalek?
It's eggs-terminated!

What do marshal arts experts eat for dinner?
Karate chops.

How do you make antifreeze?
Pinch her duvet.

How do you join the boy scouts?
Rope them all together.

Why was Cinderella no good at cricket?
She kept running away from the ball.

Who dresses in red and white, carries a huge sack and has enormous pointy teeth?
Santa Jaws.

Did you hear about the juggler who could keep a broken TV, eggshells and a copy of yesterday's newspaper in the air at the same time? That's rubbish!

How do aliens lull an alien baby to sleep? They rocket.

Did you hear about the magical Y-fronts that couldn't do tricks? They were just pants.

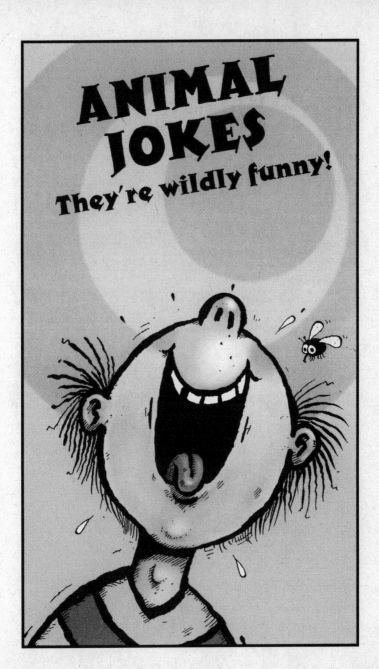

**Which type of gymnastics
are sheep best at?**
The asymmetric baaaaaas.

What's a pig's favourite ballet?
Swine Lake.

Where do milkshakes come from?
Tap-dancing cows.

What do you give a poorly pig?
Oinkment.

What do you give a horse with a cold?
Cough stirrup.

How do sheep keep warm in winter?
With central bleating.

**What happens when
kittens catch colds?**
They get cat-arrh!

Did you hear about the mean old monster who turned into a pig?
He was a swine.

Did you hear the story about the miserable bear?
It was a Grimm furry tale.

The 100 Best Brussels Sprouts Recipes
by Pa P. Bottom

Trumpet Trousers
by Warren Oise

DIY Bubble Baths
by Wynne D. Bum

It Wasn't Me
by Scarlett Cheeks

It Stinks
by Will U. Stop

Mystery Smell
by Diddy Doowit

Down the Toilet
by Sue Ridge

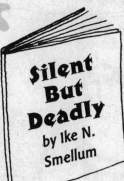

Silent But Deadly
by Ike N. Smellum

Addicted to Baked Beans
by F. R. T. Pants

What a Whiff
by Hugh Wozzit

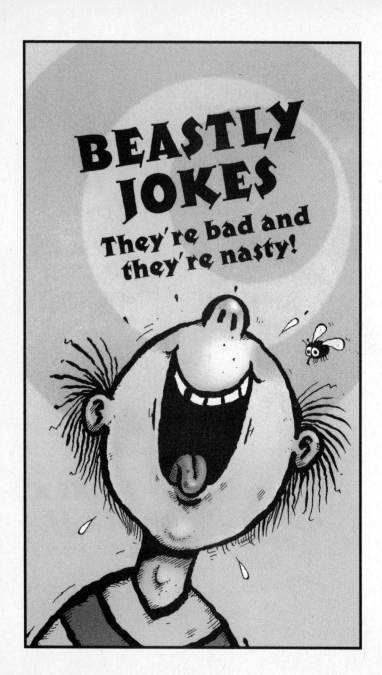

What did the cannibal say when he saw Snow White and the Seven Dwarfs?
Lunch!

What do hairy monsters eat for pudding?
Lice cream.

What flavour squash did the ogre like to slurp?
Lemon and slime.

How do monsters cook their food?
They terror-fry it.

Which soap operas do monsters love to watch?
BeastEnders and Coronation Screech.

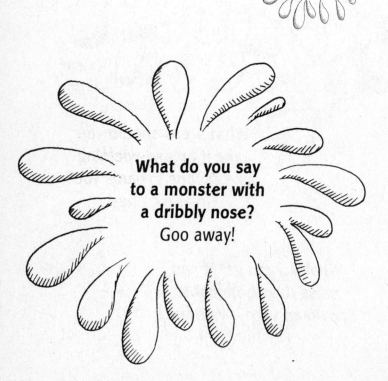

What do you say to a monster with a dribbly nose?
Goo away!

What happens when you throw a warty, stinky monster in the Dead Sea?
It gets wet.

What steps should you take if an axe-wielding ogre gallops towards you?
Great big ones!

What do you get if you cross the Abominable Snowman with a vampire?
Frostbite.

**What happens when an ogre with a big
head sits in front of you at the pictures?**
You miss most of the film.

Who won the ogres' beauty contest?
No one.

How does an ogre count to 23?
On his fingers.

Knock knock.
Who's there?
Archie.
Archie who?
Cover your nose when you sneeze, please!

Knock knock.
Who's there?
Pa.
Pa who?
Pardon me, I burped!

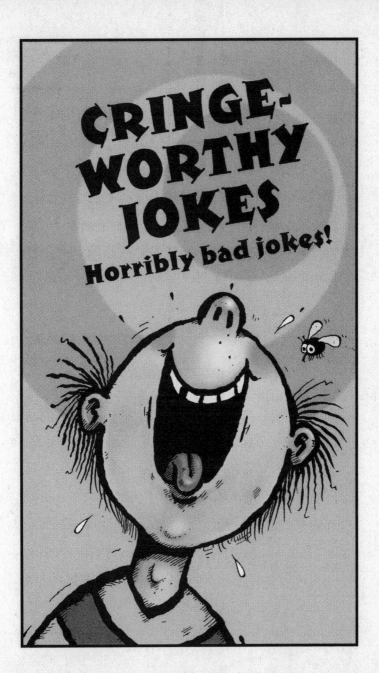

What do you call a cockerel with a gag?
A cock-a-doodle-don't.

Did you hear about the really brave turkey?
It wasn't chicken.

Why did the comedian laugh at his fried egg?
He thought it was a really funny yolk.

Did you hear the one about the speedy boiled egg?
It couldn't be beaten.

What was the egg's
favourite outfit?
A shellsuit.

Why did the chicken
carry an umbrella?
The weather was fowl.

What's hairy
and sneezes?
A coconut with
a cold.

When is a hot
vegetable not a
hot vegetable?
When it's a chilli.

Why do golf players
wear two jumpers?
In case they get a
hole in one.

Why was Shakespeare buried in Stratford-upon-Avon? Because he was dead.

What do you call someone who sits in a doctor's waiting room for hours and hours? Patient.

What kind of stories do sailors' children listen to at bedtime? Ferry tales.

What was the maths teacher's favourite meal?
Pi.

What do karate experts catch in wintertime?
Kung-flu.

What do you call a man with a seagull on his head?
Cliff.

How do you make a sausage roll?
Push it down a hill.

**What does a magician
keep up his sleeve?**
His arm!

What's green and
hairy and goes up
and down?
A gooseberry in a lift.

When is it bad luck
if a black cat
crosses your path?
When you're
a mouse.

What's black
and white and
red all over?
A penguin with
a rash.

Which king invented fractions? Henry the 1/8.

What's big, red and eats rocks? A big, red rock-eater.

What noise do hedgehogs make when they kiss? Ouch!

What's black and white and very noisy?
A panda with a drumkit.

What's black and white and black and white and black and white?
A zebra stuck in a revolving door.

Why shouldn't you ice skate on a full stomach? Because it's easier to ice skate on an ice rink.

When is a car not a car? When it turns into a garage.

Did you hear about the girl who was tap dancing? She slipped and fell into the sink.

What do you call a boy with his head down the toilet?
Huey.

What's the stickiest type of tree?
Tree-cle.

What has four wheels and flies?
A bin lorry.

What lies on the ground, a thousand feet in the air?
A millipede.

If a greengrocer had seventeen Brussels sprouts in one hand and fifteen Brussels sprouts in the other, what would he have?
Big hands!

What do you call a girl with a frog in her hair?
Lily.

**Why did the chicken
cross the road?**
To get to the other side.

**Why did the gooey
chewing gum
cross the road?**
It was stuck to the
chicken's foot.

**Why did the squashed
tomato cross the road?**
Because it was trying to
ketchup with the chicken.

**Why did the dinosaur
cross the road?**
Because it was 65 million
years BC and chickens
didn't exist.

**Why wouldn't the skeleton
cross the road?**
He didn't have the guts.

**What do you call the snail
that crossed the road?**
Lucky.

**Why did the squirrel cross
the road?**
To show the other squirrel
that he had guts.

**Why did the chicken cross
the playground?**
To get to the other slide.

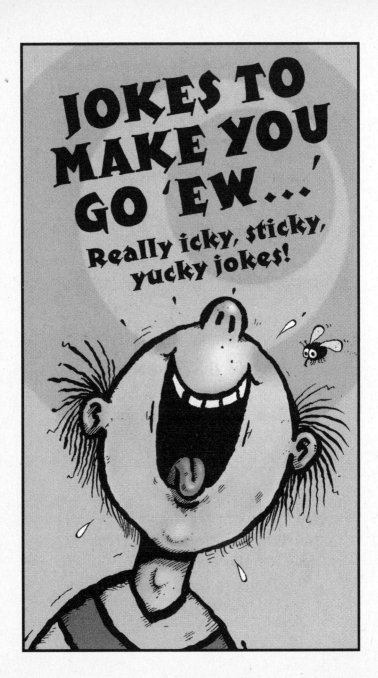

What happened when the chicken ate a big pile of sage, onion and breadcrumbs?
It was stuffed.

What happens when you take the yolk out of an egg?
It's all white.

What's loud, sticky and made of phlegm?
A cough sweet.

**Why did the monster leave a
dirty ring round the bath?**
It was just scum.

**Why shouldn't twenty seven-
year-olds pick their noses?**
Just think how many bogies
would be up twenty noses!

What happened when the bogey was flicked at a wall?
It came to a sticky end.

What did the man say when he swallowed a big, fat, juicy maggot?
Delicious grub!

Which part of the loaf did the boy with scabby knees choose?
He picked the crust.

What do you call a snail
with a housing problem?
A slug.

Why shouldn't you have Great-
uncle Bernard for dinner?
He'd be far too chewy.

What do you call a cat
that's yellow and weeps?
Pus.

Slug: Why is there a girl sitting
on your back?
Snail: That's not just any old
girl – that's Michelle.

What colour do icky sticky monsters paint their bedrooms?
Slime green.

What's yellow, gloopy and very dangerous?
Shark-infested custard.

What do you call a terribly polite child who steps in syrup?
Gooey-Two-Shoes.

What's green and wobbly and has a trunk?
A seasick tourist.

What do you call someone who likes to pick his nose under the bed?
The bogeyman.

**Where do you find
giant bogeys?**
Up giants' noses.

**How did the snail keep its
shell so shiny?**
With snail varnish.

**Did you hear about the man
who used his intestines as a
bungee rope?**
He was gutsy.

**Why did the vegetarian
take an instant dislike
to the haggis?**
It was offal.

**What's worse
than finding a
worm in your
apple?**
Finding half a
worm in your
apple.

**What's green and red
and goes round and
round and round?**
A frog in a blender.

**Which scary creature clings to the
end of your finger and won't let go?**
The bogeyman.

**What's a flea's favourite
way to travel?**
Itch-hiking.

**What do you call a fairy who
is allergic to soap and water?**
Stinkerbell.

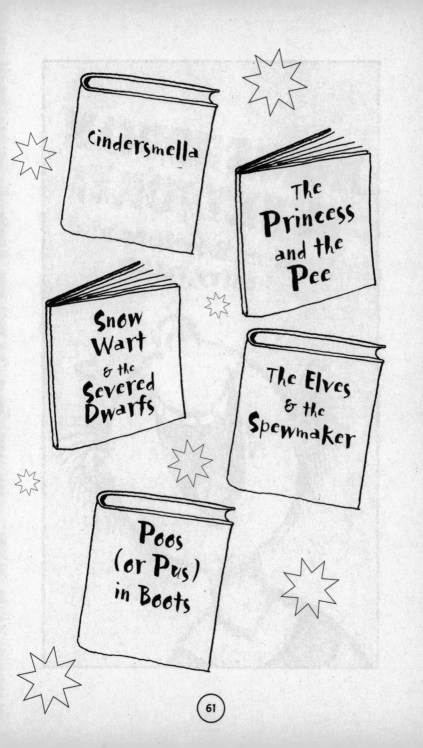

Cindersmella

The Princess and the Pee

Snow Wart & the Severed Dwarfs

The Elves & the Spewmaker

Poos (or Pus) in Boots

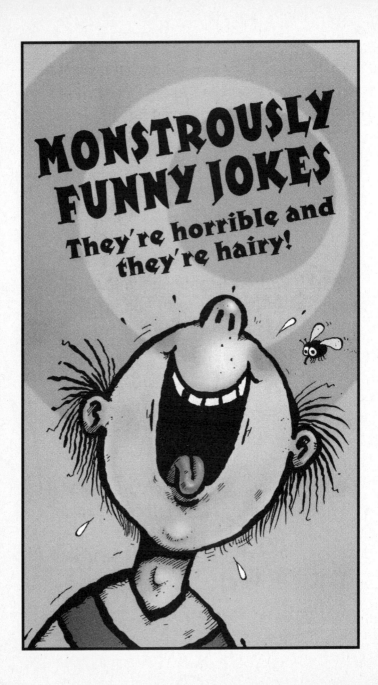

Which film do snot monsters watch on television every Christmas?
The Sound of Mucus.

Which sculpture came last in the snowman-building competition?
The Abominable Snowman.

What do you call a three-headed monster with stinky cheese in all six of his hairy ears?
Anything you like – he can't hear you!

What's green and goes boingggg? An alien on a bungee rope.

What kind of monster loves to dance? The boogieman.

What did the girl say when the monster doctor asked to look inside her mouth? Arrrrrgggghhhhh!

**What do you shout when the
Abominable Snowman surprises you?**
Not Yeti....!

**What's the best way to
speak to a monster?**
From a long way away!

**What did the monster say when he
accidentally sat on the packet of biscuits?**

Crumbs!

Where do zombies go on holiday?
The Deaditerranean.

**What is the Loch Ness Monster's
favourite takeaway meal?**
Fish 'n' ships.

**What does a monster become
after it's a year old?**
Two years old.

**Why do dragons
sleep all day?**
So that they can fight
knights!

**What do monsters eat
for pudding?**
Eyes-cream.

**Why don't monsters eat
nuclear power stations?**
They give them atomic-ache.

What's the difference between a flesh-eating sea monster and a goldfish?
Try fitting a flesh-eating sea monster into a goldfish bowl.

How did the Hunchback of Notre Dame cure his sore throat?
He gargoyled.

What time is it when a monster sits on your bike?
Time to get a new bike.

What do you say when you meet a three-headed monster?
Hello hello hello!

What do monster mums do with cars, buses and trucks?
They make traffic jam.

What goes ha ha ha THUD?
A monster laughing his head off.

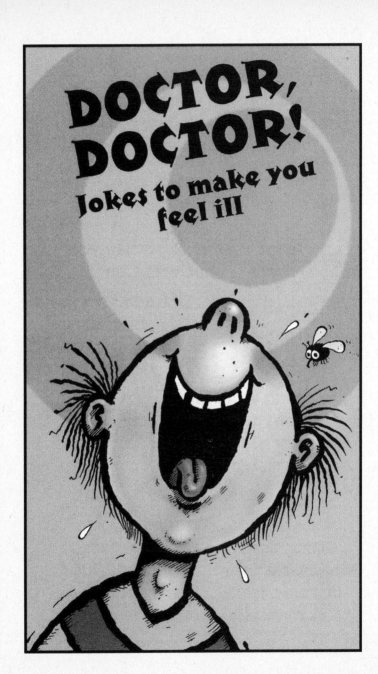

**Doctor, doctor, my
nose is running.**
No, it's snot.

**Doctor, doctor, my
nose is still running.**
Well, run after it, then!

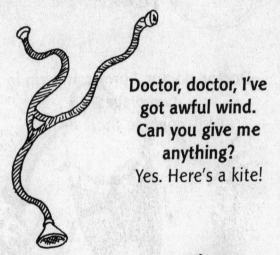

**Doctor, doctor, I've
got awful wind.
Can you give me
anything?**
Yes. Here's a kite!

**Doctor, doctor,
I keep imagining
that I'm a leech.**
Go away, sucker!

Doctor, doctor, can you help me out?
Of course. The exit's just over there.

Doctor, doctor, I broke my arm in two places...
Well, don't go there again!

Doctor, doctor, I think I'm a bridge.
What's come over you?
Eight cars, two lorries and a double-decker bus.

Why did the haunted jelly fly round in a circle?
He was doing a gloop-the-gloop.

What do you call a wizard with a furry face and a lightning-shaped scar?
Hairy Potter.

What do you call a wizard with a furry face and a lightning-shaped scar who shouts 'boo'?
Hairy Scary Potter.

What do you call a blood-sucking vampire who tells fantastic jokes?
Horribly funny.

What do you call a vampire who likes to relax in a bloodbath with a good book?
Well red.

Where do vampires keep their savings?
In a bloodbank.

Did you hear about the vampire who needed a drink?
He was bloodthirsty.

Why do vampires like thick books?
They like a story they can really get their teeth into.

Why are skeletons so lazy?
They're bone idle.

How do ghosts check that their paintings hang straight?
With a spirit level.

Why was there a road into the cemetery, but no road out of it?
It was a dead end.

How do ghost hunters keep in touch?
By eeeeeek-mail.

Why was the young ghost's birthday party so noisy?
His friends gave him the bumps in the night.

Did you hear about the really rotten spook?
He was a ghastly ghost.

How can you tell when a ghost is scared?
It goes as white as a sheet.

What do short-sighted ghosts wear?
Spooktacles.

Which part of a roast pork dinner do witches like best?
The crackling.

What happens when a ghost gets a fright?
He jumps into his skin.

Did you hear about the ghostly comedian?
He was dead funny.

Why was the bowl of soup so scary?
It was scream of tomato.

Why can't ghosts tell fibs?
Because you can see right through them.

What do you call a ghost with an upset stomach?
Spew-ky!

**Which scary creature is
always getting lost?**
A where-wolf.

**What's the scariest,
squidgiest day of
the year?**
Marshmalloween.

Why did the alien land on the roof?
Someone left the landing light on.

How did Dracula play tennis?
With a vampire bat.

What happened at the cannibals' wedding?
They toasted the bride and groom.

What did the hedgehog have to say after being trapped in the freezer?
It was a spine-chilling tale...

Why did the man's wig fly off his head at the end of the rollercoaster?

It had been a hair-raising ride.

What fruit do vampires like to munch?
Necktarines.

How can you tell when a vampire catches a cold?
Because of the coffin.

What happened when the ghouls bumped into each other at the Halloween Ball?
It was love at first fright.

Where do vampires spend their holidays?
On the Isle of Fright.

What would you find at a picnic on a haunted beach?
A sandwitch.

What do witches eat at teatime?
Spooketti.

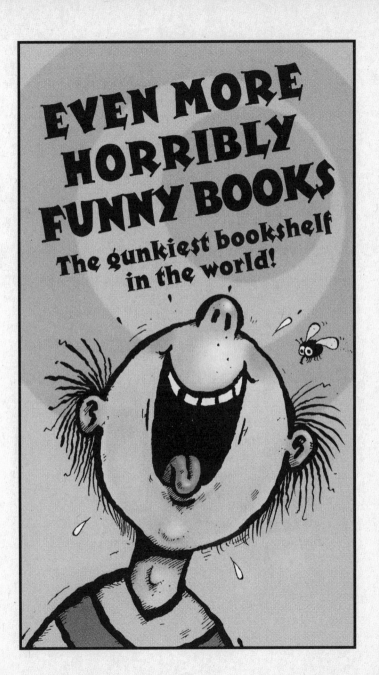

Sticky, Crusty, Yellow Gunk
by E. R. Wax

It Came From Up Her Nose
by Luke Attit

Monsters Under the Bed
by R. Maffrayed

Wipe it Clean
by Lou Seat

The Good Bogey Guide
by Chris P. Wonz

Flicking Bogies
by Megan A. Mess

Catching Monsters
by Ivor Bignette

Furry Hooters and Schnozzles of Germany and Austria
by Herr E. Nose

Smelly Shoes
by Ming Infeet

Ghost-spotting at the Seaside
by I. Screem

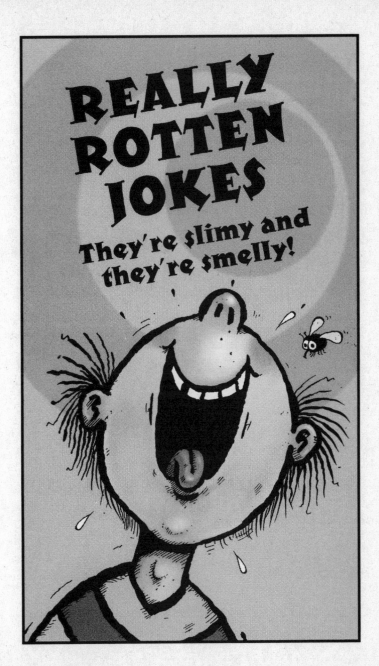

What happened when the sickly cricketer bowled the ball?
He couldn't help throwing up.

What happened when the gardener picked his nose?
He got green fingers.

Which is the stinkiest children's book character?
Winnie-the-Poo.

**Why did the mouldy
cheese disappear?**
It had gone off.

Which safari animal is really stinky?
A smellephant.

**Why did the comedy
mushroom go mouldy?**
Because he was a fun-gi.

What's the smelliest sport in the world?
Ping pong!

What did the scientist say when he discovered how to make a stink bomb?
Eww-reek-argh!

Why did the skunks start a fight?
Because they wanted to kick up a stink.

What do you call an exhausted man with a cow pat on his head?
Pooped.

What did the fisherman say to the vet?
Here's that sick squid I owe you.

What's the smelliest city in the world?
Phew York!

How many rotten eggs do you need to stink out a classroom?
A phew!

Why are bad eggs dreadful comedians?
They have such rotten yolks.

 Why was the sand wet?
Because the sea weed!

**How do you make a
teacher stew?**
Turn up late for school.

I have a warty
hooked nose,
flappy ears,
beady eyes, no
teeth and a
hairy chin.
What am I?
Ugly.

**I have a warty hooked nose, flappy ears,
beady eyes, no teeth, a hairy chin and I'm
frozen to the spot. What am I?**
Still ugly.

How do fish 'n' chip shops mistreat fish?
They batter them.

Why did the filthy burglar jump in the shower?
He wanted to make a clean getaway.

Did you hear about the clock tower that was filled with rancid cheese?
It ponged every hour.